SESAME STREET®

Celebrating YOU and ME

Many Ways to Be a
FRIEND

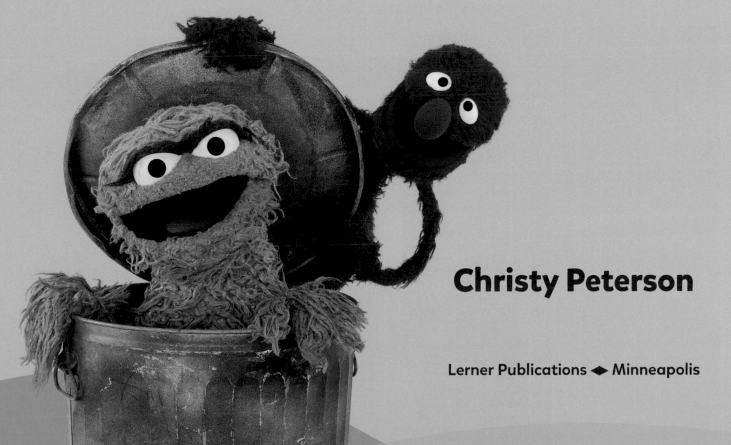

Christy Peterson

Lerner Publications ◆ Minneapolis

On Sesame Street, we celebrate everyone!

In this series, readers will explore the different ways we eat, dress, play, and more. Recognizing our similarities and differences will teach little ones to be proud of themselves and appreciate the world around them. Together, we can all be smarter, stronger, and kinder.

Sincerely, the Editors at Sesame Workshop

Table of Contents

Many Ways to Be a Friend

A friend is someone you care for and who cares for you. A friend is someone you like to spend time with.

Snuffy and I like to spend time together.

Big Bird is my best friend.

Friends can be people you have known for a long time. They can also be people you have just met.

Sometimes friends live near each other.
Other friends live far apart.

My friends in Mexico live far away. We send cards to each other.

9

Friends like to do things together.
Sometimes they do things differently.

Abby and I like to
dance together.

But we like to do
different dance
moves.

Sometimes friends like to play loudly.

Rosita and I like to play our instruments.

Sometimes friends play quietly.

**Julia and I like to sit
and read books.**

There are all different kinds of friends.
Sometimes friends aren't people!

Slimey's one of my best friends. He doesn't mind when I'm grouchy.

Friends can come from different places and look different from each other.

Sometimes we like the same things. Sometimes we like different things. And we always care for each other.

Every friend on Sesame Street is special.

Proud to Be Me!

Grab a sheet of paper and some crayons or markers. Draw a picture of you and one of your friends and give it to them.

Thanks, Tamir!

Glossary

agree: having the same opinion about something

care: to feel interest or concern

different: not the same

special: unique

Learn More

Murray, Julie. *Friendship*. Minneapolis: Abdo Kids, 2020.

Peterson, Christy. *Many Ways to Be a Family*. Minneapolis: Lerner Publications, 2023.

Rotner, Shelley, and Sheila M. Kelly. *All Kinds of Friends*. Minneapolis: Millbrook, 2018.

Index

For Erik

Photo Acknowledgments

Image credits: Ariel Skelley/DigitalVision /Getty Images, p. 4 (top); Images By Tang Ming Tung/Getty Images, p. 4 (bottom left); Richard Hutchings/Getty Images, p. 4 (bottom right); Gideon Mendel/Getty Images, pp. 6-7; Alistair Berg/DigitalVision/Getty Images, p. 8; ESB Professional/Shutterstock.com, p. 9; Monkey Business Images/Shutterstock.com, pp. 10, 18 (top); Nick David/ Getty Images, p. 14; BearFotos/Shutterstock.com, pp. 16-17; Jose Luis Pelaez Inc/DigitalVision/Getty Images, p. 18 (bottom left); FatCamera/Getty Images, p. 18 (bottom right).

Cover: FatCamera/Getty Images; thebigland/Shutterstock.com; WhitneyLewisPhotography/Getty Images.

Lerner Publications Company
An imprint of Lerner Publishing Group, Inc.
241 First Avenue North
Minneapolis, MN 55401 USA

For reading levels and more information, look up this title at www.lernerbooks.com.

Main body text set in Mikado. Typeface provided by HVD.

Editor: Amber Ross **Designer:** Laura Otto Rinne
Lerner team: Martha Kranes

Library of Congress Cataloging-in-Publication Data

Names: Peterson, Christy, author.
Title: Many ways to be a friend / Christy Peterson.
Description: Minneapolis, MN : Lerner Publications , [2023] | Series: Sesame Street celebrating you and me | Includes bibliographical references and index. | Audience: Ages 4-8 | Audience: Grades K-1 | Summary: "Friends don't have to live near one another nor do they have to like the same things. Join the Sesame Street gang as they celebrate the many ways to be a friend"— Provided by publisher.
Identifiers: LCCN 2021045349 (print) | LCCN 2021045350 (ebook) | ISBN 9781728456164 (library binding) | ISBN 9781728463711 (paperback) | ISBN 9781728462066 (ebook)
Subjects: LCSH: Friendship—Juvenile literature. | Interpersonal relations—Juvenile literature.
Classification: LCC BF575.F66 P448 2023 (print) | LCC BF575.F66 (ebook) | DDC 155.9/25—dc23/eng/20211202

LC record available at https://lccn.loc.gov/2021045349
LC ebook record available at https://lccn.loc.gov/2021045350

Manufactured in the United States of America
1-50686-50105-12/1/2021